The Future of NATO

COUNCIL *on*
FOREIGN
RELATIONS

International Institutions and
Global Governance Program

Council Special Report No. 51
February 2010

James M. Goldgeier

The Future of NATO

The Council on Foreign Relations (CFR) is an independent, nonpartisan membership organization, think tank, and publisher dedicated to being a resource for its members, government officials, business executives, journalists, educators and students, civic and religious leaders, and other interested citizens in order to help them better understand the world and the foreign policy choices facing the United States and other countries. Founded in 1921, CFR carries out its mission by maintaining a diverse membership, with special programs to promote interest and develop expertise in the next generation of foreign policy leaders; convening meetings at its headquarters in New York and in Washington, DC, and other cities where senior government officials, members of Congress, global leaders, and prominent thinkers come together with Council members to discuss and debate major international issues; supporting a Studies Program that fosters independent research, enabling CFR scholars to produce articles, reports, and books and hold round-tables that analyze foreign policy issues and make concrete policy recommendations; publishing *Foreign Affairs*, the preeminent journal on international affairs and U.S. foreign policy; sponsoring Independent Task Forces that produce reports with both findings and policy prescriptions on the most important foreign policy topics; and providing up-to-date information and analysis about world events and American foreign policy on its website, CFR.org.

The Council on Foreign Relations takes no institutional position on policy issues and has no affiliation with the U.S. government. All statements of fact and expressions of opinion contained in its publications are the sole responsibility of the author or authors.

Council Special Reports (CSRs) are concise policy briefs, produced to provide a rapid response to a developing crisis or contribute to the public's understanding of current policy dilemmas. CSRs are written by individual authors—who may be CFR fellows or acknowledged experts from outside the institution—in consultation with an advisory committee, and are intended to take sixty days from inception to publication. The committee serves as a sounding board and provides feedback on a draft report. It usually meets twice—once before a draft is written and once again when there is a draft for review; however, advisory committee members, unlike Task Force members, are not asked to sign off on the report or to otherwise endorse it. Once published, CSRs are posted on www.cfr.org.

For further information about CFR or this Special Report, please write to the Council on Foreign Relations, 58 East 68th Street, New York, NY 10065, or call the Communications office at 212.434.9888. Visit our website, CFR.org.

To submit a letter in response to a Council Special Report for publication on our website, CFR.org, you may send an email to CSReditor@cfr.org. Alternatively, letters may be mailed to us at: Publications Department, Council on Foreign Relations, 58 East 68th Street, New York, NY 10065. Letters should include the writer's name, postal address, and daytime phone number. Letters may be edited for length and clarity, and may be published online. Please do not send attachments. All letters become the property of the Council on Foreign Relations and will not be returned. We regret that, owing to the volume of correspondence, we cannot respond to every letter.

This report is printed on paper that is certified by SmartWood to the standards of the Forest Stewardship Council, which promotes environmentally responsible, socially beneficial, and economically viable management of the world's forests.

Contents

Foreword

When NATO's founding members signed the North Atlantic Treaty on April 4, 1949, they declared themselves "resolved to unite their efforts for collective defense and for the preservation of peace and security." The greatest threat to these objectives was a military attack by a hostile power—a prospect that led to the treaty's most famous provision, Article V, which states, "The Parties agree that an armed attack against one or more of them in Europe or North America shall be considered an attack against them all."

Today, more than sixty years later, the threats facing the alliance's members have changed considerably. An attack in North America or Europe by the regular army of an outside state is highly unlikely. Instead, the alliance must confront an array of more diffuse challenges, ranging from terrorism and nuclear proliferation to piracy, cyberattacks, and the disruption of energy supplies.

In this Council Special Report, James M. Goldgeier takes on the question of how NATO, having successfully kept the peace in Europe in the twentieth century, can adapt to the challenges of the twenty-first. Goldgeier contends that NATO retains value for the United States and Europe. He writes, though, that it must expand its vision of collective defense in order to remain relevant and effective. This means recognizing the full range of threats that confront NATO members today and affirming that the alliance will respond collectively to an act (whether by an outside state or a nonstate entity) that imperils the political or economic security or territorial integrity of a member state.

A central part of this debate concerns NATO's involvement in conflicts outside of Europe, including today in Afghanistan. Analyzing the questions surrounding this involvement, Goldgeier rejects any distinction between traditional Article V threats and those to be found outside the North Atlantic treaty area. Instead, he argues, these threats can be one and the same. If NATO is unable to recognize this reality and confront dangers wherever they arise, Goldgeier contends, American interest in the alliance will wane.

Examining a range of other issues, the report argues that NATO should expand its cooperation with non-European democracies, such as Australia and Japan; outlines steps to improve NATO's relations with Russia; and urges greater cooperation between NATO and the European Union. Finally, on the issue of enlargement, the report supports the current policy of keeping the door open to Georgia and Ukraine while recognizing that they will not join the alliance anytime soon.

NATO has been a cornerstone of security in Europe—and of U.S. foreign policy—for six decades. But its ability to continue playing such a central role is unclear. *The Future of NATO* takes a sober look at what the alliance and its members must do to maintain NATO's relevance in the face of today's strategic environment. The result is an important work that combines useful analysis and practical recommendations for policymakers on both sides of the Atlantic.

Richard N. Haass
President
Council on Foreign Relations
February 2010

Acknowledgments

I am grateful to this report's advisory committee members for generously lending their expertise and providing critical input. I am also grateful to CFR President Richard N. Haass and Director of Studies James M. Lindsay for their guidance and support. In addition, I received helpful advice along the way from Kaysie Brown, Jeffrey Kopstein, Tod Lindberg, Victoria Nuland, Robert Rauchhaus, Kori Schake, Anya Schmemann, and Mark Sheetz. Lucy Dunderdale, Morgan Kaplan, Josh Kvernen, Megan Liaboe, and Katy Robinette provided research support, as did Conor Savoy, who also helped shepherd the project and offered valuable suggestions for crafting the final product. I thank CFR Program Associate Andrew Lim and the Publications staff, Patricia Dorff and Lia Norton, for their assistance. Numerous officials in Washington and Brussels generously shared their time and insights with me, for which I am grateful. The German Marshall Fund of the United States and the Robina Foundation provided generous financial support. This report was crafted under the auspices of CFR's International Institutions and Global Governance program, led by Stewart M. Patrick, who helped tremendously as an adviser, editor, and friend. I thank all of them, none of whom bears responsibility for whatever flaws remain.

James M. Goldgeier

Council Special Report

Introduction

If the North Atlantic Treaty Organization (NATO) did not exist today, the United States would not seek to create it. In 1949, it made sense in the face of a potential Soviet invasion to forge a bond in the North Atlantic area among the United States, Canada, and the west European states. Today, if the United States were starting from scratch in a world of transnational threats, the debate would be over whether to follow liberal and neoconservative calls for an alliance of democracies without regard to geography or to develop a great power concert envisioned by the realists to uphold the current order.

The United States is not, however, starting from scratch, and NATO should not disappear. While the bonds across the Atlantic may be frayed, they are stronger than those tying the United States to other parts of the world. Common history and values matter, as do the resources (both financial and military) that Europe possesses. The NATO allies share a common interest in preventing disruptions to the global economy, including attacks on freedom of navigation. As a community of democracies, the member states are threatened by forces such as Islamic extremism and the rise of authoritarian states. For the United States, the alliance is a source of legitimacy for actions in places like Afghanistan. For Europe, NATO is a vehicle for projecting hard power. While NATO alone cannot defend against the range of threats facing the member states, it can serve as the hub for American and European leaders to develop the ties with other institutions and non-European countries necessary to provide for the common defense. For all its faults, NATO enables the United States to partner with close democratic allies in ways that would be difficult without a formal institution that provides a headquarters and ready venue for decision-making, as well as legitimacy and support for action that ad hoc U.S.-led coalitions do not.

As has been true since the fall of the Berlin Wall two decades ago, the United States (and Europe) should want NATO to succeed. After the Cold War, the alliance dramatically redefined itself. In the 1990s, it fostered stability across Europe by beginning its process of enlargement to the formerly communist east and by intervening to stop genocide in the Balkans. In the 2000s, it broadened its scope through the mission in Afghanistan as well as a counterterrorist operation in the Mediterranean and counterpiracy efforts in the Gulf of Aden and off the Horn of Africa (in addition to continuing the enlargement process). But as NATO has broadened its scope, some members have grown concerned that the alliance is shifting its attention away from Europe. These members seek to return NATO to a more traditional understanding of its role defending against threats on the continent, particularly as an increasingly authoritarian and assertive Russian government has sought to reclaim a sphere of influence lost in the Soviet collapse.

In November 2010, NATO will release a new "strategic concept" to guide the alliance going forward. That document must state clearly that providing for collective defense in the twenty-first century goes well beyond defending against the "armed attack" of Article V. To remain relevant, NATO must expand its traditional understanding of collective defense to confront the twenty-first-century threats of terrorism, proliferation of weapons of mass destruction (WMD) to both states and nonstate actors, and cyberwarfare. By necessity, the United States has turned its attention away from Europe in order to counter these modern threats, which largely emanate from Africa, the broader Middle East, and Asia. If NATO fails to accept a growing global role, then the United States will lose interest in investing in the alliance's future. But Europe faces these threats too and must recognize that a more robust NATO offers it the chance to counter them. Given the varied nature and source of threats today, NATO can be successful only if the Europeans agree to stronger NATO-European Union (EU) cooperation and to closer ties with major non-European democracies, particularly those in the Asia-Pacific region.

Looking to the threats of the past, NATO still needs to provide assurance to its east European members that remain wary of Russia's intentions. The strategic concept offers NATO the opportunity to reaffirm its commitment to Article V—an attack on one is an attack on all. However, the strategic concept must also clarify the alliance's relationship with Russia. In addition to providing assurance to member states, NATO must work to improve its relationship with Russia. Ultimately, improved relations with Russia will do more to address eastern European fears than contingency planning and military exercises. But a better relationship with Moscow is also necessary in a world of transnational threats. Although NATO is a values-based institution, collaboration among the world's democracies is simply not sufficient to combat threats like terrorism and proliferation. Russia and NATO are no longer enemies; it is time to form a productive partnership between the two.

Much rests on the upcoming strategic concept. It is an important opportunity for the alliance to provide assurance that the bedrock of NATO—Article V—remains sacrosanct but also to broaden the institution's scope to respond to new challenges. A Europe largely at peace and secure within its borders is one of the most important results of the end of the Cold War and represents an opportunity for both the United States and Europe to turn their attention to the threats arising elsewhere.

NATO's Purpose: Collective Defense in the Twenty-first Century

Since the end of the Cold War, NATO has defined itself through its military response to "out-of-area" conflicts, first in Bosnia, then in Kosovo, and now in Afghanistan. Every military action since 1995 has been more difficult than the previous one, and each time elites argued that the credibility of the alliance was at stake. Just as in the case of the Balkans in the 1990s, many argue that the credibility of the alliance rests on the success of the mission in Afghanistan. This fear for NATO's reputation sidesteps the central question: What is NATO's purpose?

The development of a new strategic concept offers NATO the opportunity to determine in principle when, where, how, and why it needs to act rather than simply responding in an ad hoc manner as new problems arise that its leaders determine require alliance action. While there will inevitably be new challenges to alliance members that require a novel response (who, after all, would have predicted the growing need to combat piracy?), the alliance has the opportunity in 2010 to provide the public with a rationale for why and how the countries of North America and Europe should respond collectively to the range of threats that face them.

In 1949, everyone understood that "an armed attack" as described in Article V of the Washington Treaty meant a Soviet land offensive in Europe. The threat was clear, and solidarity was essential. If Soviet forces swept across Germany, citizens of the Netherlands and Belgium knew they would be next. Soviet domination of the continent in turn would directly affect North America's vital interests. It was easy to believe that, as Article V declared, "an armed attack on one or more [alliance members] in Europe or North America [would be] considered an attack against them all."

That sense of solidarity is difficult, if not impossible, to re-create today. Although a number of eastern European nations developed an increasing sense of insecurity after the 2008 Russia-Georgia war, citizens in France and Portugal do not lie awake at night fearing a resurgent Red Army.

The likeliest threats to NATO members are the kinds of terrorist attacks that occurred in the United States in 2001, Istanbul in 2003, Madrid in 2004, and London in 2005. Today one hears NATO representatives talk about the need to balance Article V with the need for NATO to act as an "expeditionary alliance" (a term introduced by President George W. Bush at the 2008 Bucharest summit). But the prospect of attacks against its citizens by terrorists operating from bases in places like Afghanistan and Pakistan can pose an Article V threat, as NATO members intuitively understood immediately after the 9/11 attacks, even if many have lost that sense of purpose since. Acting as an expeditionary alliance is not secondary to Article V; in certain cases today, it is the essence of Article V.

A more difficult challenge both conceptually and practically is to articulate NATO's role in the face of nonmilitary and even nonviolent threats that can devastate a society. Russia, for example, is less likely to launch a military assault against a NATO member than it is to engage in other types of intimidation. Cyberattacks against Estonia in 2007, originating from Russian territory, were the face of a new type of warfare, and past Russian cutoffs of gas supplies that run through Ukraine have left populations in NATO countries such as Romania and Bulgaria freezing in the dark.

Are cyberattacks or energy cutoffs Article V threats? By definition they are not "armed attacks." But if the alliance is to mean anything, NATO has to band together in the face of assaults that threaten a member state. In these nonmilitary instances, NATO can invoke Article IV, which reads, "The Parties will consult together whenever, in the opinion of any of them, the territorial integrity, political independence or security of any of the Parties is threatened."

The important point is not whether a threat is better viewed as falling under Article IV or Article V; what is important is an alliance commitment that a threat to one member will be met collectively. In the strategic concept, NATO members should affirm that *any action initiated by an external state or nonstate actor that threatens the political and economic security or territorial integrity of a NATO member will engender a collective response.*

Beyond Europe

U.S. permanent representative to NATO Ivo H. Daalder has argued, "The North Atlantic area is no island. It is submerged in a globally integrated world. Today, the right lens for transatlantic relations is not so much American or European—it is global. And NATO, too, must increasingly view itself not only from a transatlantic perspective, but a global perspective."[1] Having a global perspective means not simply recognizing that threats can come from anywhere and take different forms; it means enhancing the alliance's ties with partners around the world. NATO relationships with other institutions and countries are nothing new. The alliance took over the UN-authorized International Security Assistance Force (ISAF) in Afghanistan in 2003, and established Operation Allied Provider to counter piracy after UN secretary-general Ban Ki-moon requested escorts for UN World Food Program vessels traveling near the Horn of Africa and the Gulf of Aden. The alliance created a Mediterranean Dialogue and the Istanbul Cooperation Initiative to expand its relationships with countries across the broader Middle East that participate in Partnership for Peace activities, engage in military cooperation, and exchange information.

Relatively underdeveloped, however, are the alliance's ties with the major non-NATO democracies. In 2006, then NATO secretary-general Jaap de Hoop Scheffer called on the alliance to develop closer partnerships with Australia, Finland, Japan, New Zealand, South Korea, and Sweden. A U.S. proposal to create a formal institution within NATO to build these partnerships foundered, in part because of fears by some Europeans that NATO would lose its transatlantic focus and become a tool for American military ventures around the world, but also because the six sought-after partners were not interested in such a formal arrangement.

Each partner has different aspirations. The two European nations are members of the European Union and have debated whether to pursue

NATO membership. Should they decide to do so, their inclusion in the alliance would be a foregone conclusion. None of the four Asia-Pacific democracies is likely to seek membership, a step that anyway would require revision of Article X of the NATO Treaty (which allows for the enlargement of the alliance only to European countries) and would generate huge opposition within Europe, which does not want the alliance to lose its transatlantic focus. NATO should continue to work with each Asia-Pacific partner individually to develop a pace of coordination that fits the needs of those countries through the tailored cooperation packages. These should be enhanced, and the opportunities for participation in NATO should be expanded. Australia, for example, has been a major contributor to the military mission in Afghanistan, and should be encouraged to participate more closely in the alliance's ongoing efforts at military transformation and the development of a rapid response force. In future missions, any nonmember country that provides significant military assistance—at least one thousand troops—should be part of the operational planning process, even if it has only nonvoting status in the deliberations. Japan, which recently announced greater economic assistance for Afghanistan, has also shown interest in missile defense and could contribute to the effort to protect the alliance against proliferators. These and other major non-European democracies have a huge potential role to play as the alliance retools itself to combat threats emanating from far-flung places.

The alliance can put these partnerships in the proper context only if it recognizes the breadth and depth of the current threat environment. If NATO's sole purpose is to ensure security within Europe through the U.S. commitment to the continent, then these partnerships are peripheral. If the purpose of the alliance is to deal with global challenges, then the partners become central.

NATO's success has depended on the shared values that underpin the alliance. As NATO looks for external partners, it should focus on closer ties to non-European democracies. But while NATO's natural partners are democratic, it faces challenges—such as counterterrorism and counterproliferation—that will require collaboration with non-democracies. First and foremost, that means cooperating with Russia.

NATO and Russia

The core problem in NATO-Russia relations can be summed up quite simply: NATO will not allow Russia to have a veto over alliance decisions, while Russia believes it is a great power deserving a full voice in European security affairs. Because NATO has been able to pursue policies despite Russian objections, it has done so, breeding further resentment from Moscow every time. But it is more than just an issue of power; it is also a question of purpose. NATO has sought to create security and stability throughout eastern Europe. Russia, meanwhile, has sown discord and instability in places such as Ukraine, Moldova, and Georgia in order to increase its influence and prevent further encroachment by NATO. These two contrasting visions of European security lie at the heart of the differences between the West and Russia.

Russia has objected to NATO's expansion toward its territory and has viewed the policy to include the central and eastern European democracies as a humiliating effort by the United States to extend its sphere of influence at a time when Russia was weak. NATO believed that its benign intentions to expand the zone of peace and prosperity in Europe would eventually be understood and accepted in Moscow as a benefit to all, and not as a threat to Russia.

Had NATO not enlarged, the European Union likely would have delayed its own enlargement process, leaving central and eastern Europe insecure and vulnerable. Those who have opposed enlargement cite the cost of difficult relations with Russia, but they do not consider what the costs of not enlarging would have been, including the possible failure of political and economic reform in central Europe and the potential for increased conflict in the region.

The future of enlargement is uncertain. While progress continues in the Balkans (Montenegro joined the Membership Action Plan in December 2009, and NATO has affirmed its support for Bosnia and Herzegovina to do the same once it fulfills certain reforms), the prospect of Ukraine and Georgia joining the alliance will remain dim for some time to come.

NATO's current policy toward Georgian and Ukrainian membership is sound. The alliance is reviewing both countries' progress annually, allowing them to develop closer ties to NATO if they desire, and holding the door open for future membership. Each country has significant obstacles to near-term membership. Ukraine has enormous internal political challenges, and its population remains unconvinced that joining NATO is a worthy goal; meanwhile, the 2008 Russia-Georgia war ensured that the territorial dispute between those two nations will not be resolved anytime soon. Notably, at their 2009 summit, the alliance leaders declared, "NATO's door will remain open to all European democracies which share the values of our Alliance, which are willing and able to assume the responsibilities and obligations of membership, and whose inclusion can contribute to common security and stability."[2] The first two have been standard criteria throughout the post–Cold War enlargement process; enunciating the third has ensured that the hurdle is higher for Ukraine and Georgia, given their disputes with Russia, than it was for previous aspirants. President Barack Obama added an additional threshold when he was in Moscow in July 2009, stating that a majority of the population of an aspirant must support membership, a line clearly directed at Ukraine.[3]

NATO should reaffirm its openness to European states that meet its criteria to maintain the integrity of Article X and to avoid drawing unnecessary lines in Europe, but the slow path to membership for Ukraine and Georgia does lessen tensions with Moscow and open greater possibilities for cooperation with Russia, as does President Obama's decision not to deploy the Bush administration's proposed missile defense system in Poland and the Czech Republic. Instead, Obama decided to shift to a forward, sea-based system (built around Aegis-equipped warships armed with the SM-3 missile) to counter the short-range and medium-range missile threat from Iran. The new sea-based system would be based in the eastern Mediterranean (and possibly the Black Sea and Persian Gulf) to protect American allies in the region. Over time, the system may incorporate forward-based radar systems in Turkey, the Gulf region, and possibly the Caucasus, as well as land-based mobile interceptors (including in Poland). The Obama administration believes that this system is more attuned with the actual Iranian threat and provides a defense for all NATO allies. An added benefit is that it should allow for greater U.S.-Europe-Russia collaboration on missile defense that could protect against an Iranian threat. The United States should continue to seek incorporation of the Russian-operated radar site in Azerbaijan as part of a regional defense system.

The ability of NATO and the United States to collaborate with Russia will depend heavily on how Russia understands the "reset" of relations sought by the Obama administration. To date, Russia has behaved as if the reset signals an American shift on policies such as enlargement and missile defense that previously angered Moscow rather than an opportunity for both sides to rethink their approaches to problems. The Obama administration has hoped that Russia would support stiff sanctions against Iran and allow greater transit for American troops heading to Afghanistan. Each time President Dmitri Medvedev has hinted at support for tough sanctions, Prime Minister Vladimir Putin has thrown cold water on the idea. Russia has been slow to implement the transit agreement on Afghanistan signed in July 2009; Moscow has approved only a handful of flights. A core problem regarding both Iran and Afghanistan is a divergence of interests and a Russian preference for the status quo. Russia does not want Iran to develop nuclear weapons, but it also does not want a U.S.-Iran rapprochement that worsens Moscow's geostrategic position. Similarly, Russia does not want the Taliban to return to power in Afghanistan, but neither does it necessarily want American-led forces to achieve a clear victory.

A significant question for Europe is whether Russia will adhere to the provisions of the Helsinki Final Act, in particular, the prohibition on changing borders by force. Russia broke that treaty in August 2008 when it went to war to support the secession of South Ossetia and Abkhazia from Georgia. Russia's actions demonstrated the limits of the Organization for Security and Cooperation in Europe's ability to serve as a dispute settlement mechanism. They also demonstrated NATO's limits in upholding the Helsinki principles on non-NATO territory in yet another instance of the alliance being unable to manage threats on its own, as well as the failure of the NATO-Russia Council to take meaningful action.

There are no obvious answers to this problem, but in the near term, the United States should promote practical cooperation that builds greater confidence on both sides. The NATO-Russia Council appears ready to expand the number of joint exercises and training operations to deal with issues such as terrorism and nuclear safety, as has occurred periodically in recent years. If Europeans can manage to fulfill their commitments to the NATO response force, then NATO could propose a joint NATO-Russia response force to manage emergency situations across the region.

Better relations with Moscow cannot (and need not) come at the expense of the security of eastern European alliance members. NATO needs to take seriously contingency planning for the protection of the Baltic states, particularly Estonia and Latvia, while recognizing that transparency is essential to assure the Russians these efforts are purely defensive.

NATO Capabilities

In response to the new threat environment, NATO has to prepare itself for a range of military contingencies, including responding to states and groups around the world that are planning attacks on European and North American targets. Unfortunately, Europe has little capability to transport its troops across significant distances—more than 70 percent of European land forces cannot deploy. The minimal requirements the alliance set for itself to establish a NATO response force (twenty-five thousand combined land, air, and naval forces) have gone unmet, as has the provision of important equipment such as helicopters.

In addition to fulfilling the stated requirements of the response force, NATO will need to focus its attention increasingly on maritime and missile defense capabilities. Under Operation Active Endeavor, NATO ships are patrolling the Mediterranean to counter terrorism, interdict weapons of mass destruction, and mitigate threats of piracy. This Article V mission requires enhancing NATO capabilities to combat nonstate threats at sea.[4] On missile defense, President Obama's decision to focus on short- and medium-range Iranian missile capabilities has centered attention on the threats to Europe emanating from the Middle East, thus changing the missile defense discussion from how to protect the American homeland toward how to defend NATO territory. The next step is to gain allied agreement that territorial missile defense is an Article V mission, requiring the alliance as a whole, not just the United States, to contribute to the project.

As NATO prepares to respond to the nonmilitary threats to members, it must recognize that it does not have the capacity to respond by itself to these challenges. Although it has established the NATO Computer Incident Response Capability to respond to cyberaggression, for example, it has insufficient technological capabilities within the organization to respond to cyberwarfare. While NATO officials have spoken of the need to "protect critical energy infrastructure" (and Operation

Active Endeavor was established to protect the flow of oil and gas through the Mediterranean against terrorist actions), energy security is largely a political challenge.

One option for the alliance is to develop not just military but non-military capacities to deal with future contingencies. It would be preferable to work with organizations such as the European Union that have both the resources and experience to complement NATO's military role. NATO can focus on ensuring that it has the hard power necessary to deal with various threats, ranging from states developing missile and WMD capabilities to terrorists and pirates, while working closely with other institutions and even nongovernmental organizations and private corporations to resolve the nonmilitary threats facing alliance members. U.S. secretary of state Hillary Clinton has spoken of the need to move toward a "multipartner world."[5] Perhaps nowhere is that more true than for NATO.

On military matters, NATO can take the lead role, as it did in Bosnia, Kosovo, and Afghanistan, even if it eventually turns to organizations such as the EU to take over once a situation is stabilized, as was the case in the Balkans. On issues such as cyber- and energy security, the EU would ideally take the lead role, while NATO could assist with logistical support and personnel as needed to resolve problems. Given the significant overlap in membership between the two organizations, this coordination should not be difficult, but it is. Achieving the necessary cooperation will take greater willingness by the United States to develop its own relationship with the European Union, and it will take concerted effort on the part of EU members to work more closely with NATO.

NATO and the EU

Most alliance members are not going to make major military contributions. They never did and they never will. The United States will continue to press for greater burden sharing, but such efforts will be effective only at the margins.

Most NATO members, however, can add value in their capacity as part of the EU. In countering terrorism, for example, Europe has developed tools for both intelligence gathering and disrupting terrorist finances. The EU has established a Joint Situation Centre in Brussels, composed of national intelligence experts, that briefs EU policymakers on terrorist activities. It has gone far in linking national criminal databases, and is able to monitor extremists and seize financial assets of suspected criminals. The EU maintains a twenty-four-hour monitoring and information center for emergency civilian assistance in the event of a WMD attack.[6]

Enhancing the EU's partnership with NATO by allowing for more joint action is the logical place for European members of the alliance to make a greater contribution. The EU has tremendous nonmilitary resources, but it has been wary of working more closely with NATO. Many Europeans who already fear NATO is merely a tool of U.S. imperialism do not want to allow the United States to play more of a role within the European Union. The EU's recent adoption of the Lisbon Treaty, however, offers some hope for new possibilities. The treaty allows for more flexibility by a subset of EU members willing to engage in military and defense cooperation, and it also expands the scope of the EU Common Security and Defense Policy (CSDP) to "joint disarmament operations; military advice and assistance tasks, peace-making and post-conflict stabilization; conflict prevention and post-conflict stabilization missions."[7]

Although the Lisbon Treaty is an important step forward for the EU, a major obstacle to NATO-EU collaboration is the ongoing dispute between Turkey and Cyprus. Cyprus vetoed the EU commitment to end the trade blockade on Northern Cyprus; in return, Turkey reneged on its promise to open its ports to Cypriot shipping. Cyprus has blocked Turkey's participation in the EU defense agency, and Turkey will not let Cyprus work with NATO. Although working-level contacts between the two institutions are significant (e.g., there is an EU staff cell at Supreme Headquarters Allied Powers Europe [SHAPE], NATO's military headquarters), high-level interaction is minimal, and therefore so is any serious collaboration in areas such as conflict prevention and crisis management.

With the Lisbon Treaty, the EU will no longer continue to suffer as much in foreign policy from its six-month rotating presidency that left it ill-equipped to lay out strategic priorities. But the decision not to appoint visible and charismatic personalities to the positions of European president and foreign minister demonstrated that the major European countries still need to assert the leadership necessary to break the current institutional impasse between the EU and NATO.

Much U.S. concern about the large states in Europe has focused on their limited military role in Afghanistan. While it would be helpful for countries such as Germany and Italy to develop greater counterinsurgency capacity, they are unlikely to do so. It is better that they devote their energies to creating opportunities for more significant NATO-EU cooperation. Turkey, for example, wants greater access to the European Defense Agency and the CSDP before it will support greater institutional collaboration. The major European powers must find a way to make this happen. The United States, meanwhile, will have to take the lead role in reassuring Turkey that in exchange for its support for NATO operations, Ankara will not find itself isolated within the alliance.

The problem of NATO-EU cooperation goes beyond Turkey and Cyprus. Those countries that are members of both NATO and the EU have two separate foreign policies. They do not coordinate their efforts or their missions. And they do not see that as a problem.

NATO's hard power and the EU's soft power would be a potent combination. Take postconflict reconstruction and stabilization. Some have called for a NATO stabilization and reconstruction force that can work with the European Union.[8] But why duplicate capabilities? The United States and European Union can develop these capacities through their civilian agencies (as the United States has done within the

State Department) and then work jointly with NATO military planners to prepare for future postconflict situations. Franklin D. Kramer and Simon Serfaty have proposed creating a Euro-Atlantic Forum to serve as a strategic coordinator for NATO-EU actions.[9] Locating such an entity in Paris would be a good way not only to take advantage of France's return to NATO's integrated military command, but to give France an incentive to find ways to build the NATO-EU relationship.

The NATO-EU relationship will also depend on a stronger U.S.-EU relationship. The United States needs to beef up its mission to the EU and create closer ties between the staffs at its EU and NATO missions in Brussels. Currently, only one person at the U.S. mission to the EU is assigned to defense cooperation.[10] In addition to increasing the number of personnel to work on defense at the EU mission, the United States should install a deputy at both its NATO and EU missions who would be responsible for liaison with the other mission.

Conclusions

When NATO invoked Article V for the first time in its history—on September 12, 2001—Europeans conveyed their solidarity with the United States in a world in which geography and traditional territorial defense mattered less than unconventional, transnational threats. Unfortunately, today European citizens largely view the war in Afghanistan as a humanitarian operation and not as a response to a direct threat of terrorism.

In a hopeful sign for the future, NATO member states offered nearly seven thousand more troops to Afghanistan in December 2009 after President Obama's speech at West Point on the new Afghan war strategy, but the number of allies offering more troops was small, and most of those forces will not be engaged in combat operations. Two of NATO's leading members, France and Germany, disappointed the United States in the run-up to the January 2010 London Conference on Afghanistan. French president Nicolas Sarkozy reiterated that his country would not send additional troops, and Germany offered a mere 850 more. Two countries that have put troops in harm's way, the Netherlands and Canada, had previously announced that their combat troops would be withdrawn by 2010 and 2011, respectively. And given that over the course of 2009 Obama had ordered more than fifty thousand new forces to join the counterinsurgency, what was once a fairly even split in the NATO International Security Assistance Force (ISAF) mission between Americans and non-Americans was now heavily tilting in the direction of American fighting men and women. The December 2009 NATO pledge was welcome, but it was unlikely to stem growing bipartisan criticism in Washington that the alliance has not done enough.

Only a handful of members other than the United States, in particular Canada, the Netherlands, the United Kingdom, and nonmember Australia (as well as Denmark and Romania), have been willing to send their troops to dangerous areas of the south and east (although even those operating elsewhere in Afghanistan, including Italy and Germany, are suffering casualties). While reconstruction efforts and police training are necessary components of the overall mission in Afghanistan, U.S. secretary of defense Robert M. Gates has warned of the danger of NATO becoming a "two-tiered alliance of those who are willing to fight and those who are not."[11]

Although Washington would like to see Europeans do more militarily, NATO missions around the world, including those in Afghanistan, Kosovo, the Mediterranean, and the Horn of Africa, currently involve over seventy thousand military personnel. More than forty nations contribute to ISAF, and most of those would be unlikely to put troops in Afghanistan if the mission were being run under the U.S. flag.

Increasingly, NATO is training others—Iraqis, Afghans, the African Union—to provide for their own security. It has individual partnerships with more than forty nations (including more than twenty members of Partnership for Peace). Dialogue with major countries such as India and China is likely to grow stronger. Convincing European publics of NATO's role in combating global threats is the foremost challenge facing Europe's leaders, which means building a common sense of threat perception. In Afghanistan, even those European countries not able to contribute more troops have to recognize that instability in Southwest Asia poses a common threat to the members of the alliance. If they cannot develop solidarity on an issue central to the Obama administration and provide, for example, significantly more EU assistance to the region—the EU announced modest new sums recently, as did Germany and a number of other countries—then U.S. policymakers will grow increasingly disinterested in NATO as they confront real dangers outside the North Atlantic area.

Potential U.S. disinterest is the greatest danger facing NATO going forward. To keep the United States engaged in the North Atlantic Alliance, the Europeans must signal that they understand the new threat environment and what it takes to meet that threat. It would be far better for both the United States and Europe if NATO succeeds. American reassurance is still valuable within Europe. A formal institution of leading democracies that provides a forum for discussion and a vehicle for action is a significant advantage for the United States as it seeks to promote international order.

Recommendations

NATO remains valuable to both the United States and Europe, and the member states should continue to invest in the alliance.

NATO provides the United States with legitimacy for action that does not accrue to coalitions of the willing, and it allows the Europeans to project power in a way that they cannot do on their own.

NATO must recognize that Article V's pledge that an "armed attack" on one shall be considered an attack on all is insufficient to defend its members against the range of threats that can undermine the national security of member states. In the strategic concept, NATO members should affirm that any action initiated by an external state or nonstate actor that threatens the political and economic security or the territorial integrity of a NATO member requires a collective response through Article IV or Article V.

These potential threats to security include a terrorist or missile attack, an external effort to topple a regime or occupy territory, a cyberassault that threatens to paralyze a nation's political and/or economic infrastructure, or a cutoff of energy supplies.

NATO members must also recognize that Article V threats can arise from outside the continent. The issue is not "Article V versus expeditionary"; the issue is how to respond to common threats to security regardless of their origin. If it fails to do so, the alliance will lose its central role in American national security policy.

NATO should strengthen its partnerships with the EU and with non-European democracies.

To ensure the resources necessary to respond to nonmilitary threats, the United States should push those European nations that are members of both NATO and the EU to help break down the barriers to cooperation between the two institutions to allow for more joint action, particularly in the areas of conflict prevention and crisis management.

European partners should promote Turkish access to the European Defense Agency and the European Security and Defense Policy in order to help mitigate the obstacles to EU-NATO collaboration.

The United States should strengthen its mission to the EU, particularly by adding personnel to work on defense cooperation and ensure that the American missions to the EU and NATO are working closely together. It should install a deputy at each mission responsible for liaison with the other mission.

Locating an EU-NATO institutional forum for cooperation in Paris would take advantage of France's return to NATO's integrated military command and give France an incentive to find ways to build a stronger EU-NATO partnership.

In a world of global threats, NATO must enhance its ties with partners around the world, including the major Asia-Pacific democracies, by providing opportunities for more collaboration at NATO headquarters and at SHAPE for those partners in areas such as missile defense and the crisis response force. An alliance that sees itself merely as transatlantic in focus is an anachronism of the twentieth century, when the threats to Europe came from Europe, and when there were few democracies outside the region.

As Australia has demonstrated, nonmember nations can provide important military contributions. In any future mission in which a nonmember provides significant military assistance—at least one thousand troops—that country should be part of the operational planning process, even if it only has nonvoting status in the deliberations.

To be relevant to future threats, NATO will need to focus its attention increasingly on developing maritime and missile defense capabilities.

The United States should foster greater collaboration between NATO and Russia.

The United States should promote practical cooperation that might build greater confidence between the alliance and Russia. The NATO-Russia Council should expand the joint exercises and training operations to deal with issues such as terrorism and nuclear safety. And if Europeans can manage to fulfill their commitments to the NATO response force, then NATO could propose a joint NATO-Russia response force to manage emergency situations across the region.

The Obama administration's missile defense decision opens the opportunity for collaboration with Russia, including joint assessments of the missile threat from Iran. The United States should actively seek Russian partnership in a joint missile defense.

At the same time, NATO needs to reassure east European alliance members that Article V ensures their defense against Russian intimidation. That means that NATO needs to take seriously contingency planning for the protection of the Baltic states, particularly Estonia and Latvia. NATO should also reaffirm its commitment to its open-door policy on enlargement in Europe and maintain its current policy of an annual review for Georgia and Ukraine.

Endnotes

1. Ambassador Ivo H. Daalder, permanent representative of the United States to NATO, Transatlantic Forum, Berlin, July 1, 2009, http://nato.usmission.gov/Speeches/Daalder_FA_Berlin070109.asp.

2. The 2009 NATO summit declaration on alliance security, http://www.nato.int/cps/en/natolive/news_52838.htm?mode=pressrelease.

3. "Remarks by the President at the New Economic School Graduation," Gostinny Dvor, Moscow, Russia, the White House, Office of the Press Secretary, July 7, 2009, http://www.whitehouse.gov/the_press_office/REMARKS-BY-THE-PRESIDENT-AT-THE-NEW-ECONOMIC-SCHOOL-GRADUATION/.

4. A good first step is NATO's Comprehensive, Strategic-Level Policy for Preventing the Proliferation of Weapons of Mass Destruction (WMD) and Defending Against Chemical, Biological, Radiological and Nuclear (CBRN) Threats.

5. Hillary Rodham Clinton, foreign policy address at the Council on Foreign Relations, July 15, 2009, http://www.state.gov/secretary/rm/2009a/july/126071.htm.

6. Hugo Brady, "Intelligence, Emergencies, and Foreign Policy: The EU's Role in Counterterrorism," Centre for European Reform, July 2009.

7. See Daniel S. Hamilton, Testimony to the House Committee on Foreign Affairs, Subcommittee on Europe, "The Lisbon Treaty: Implications for Future Relations Between the European Union and the United States," December 15, 2009.

8. Daniel Hamilton et al., "Alliance Report: An Atlantic Compact of the 21st Century," Report of the Atlantic Council of the United States, Center for Strategic & International Studies, Center for Technology and National Security Policy at NDU, and Center for Transatlantic Relations at Johns Hopkins University, SAIS, February 2009, p. ix.

9. Franklin D. Kramer and Simon Serfaty, "Recasting the Euro-Atlantic Partnership," Initiative for a Renewed Transatlantic Partnership, Center for Strategic & International Studies, February 1, 2007, p. iii.

10. Hamilton, Testimony to the House Committee on Foreign Affairs, December 15, 2009.

11. Defense Secretary Robert M. Gates, Munich Conference on Security Policy in Munich, Germany, February 10, 2008, http://www.defenselink.mil/speeches/speech.aspx?speechid=1214.

About the Author

James M. Goldgeier is the Whitney Shepardson senior fellow for transatlantic relations at the Council on Foreign Relations and coauthor of *America Between the Wars: From 11/9 to 9/11*. He was previously an adjunct senior fellow for Europe studies at CFR and the Henry A. Kissinger scholar in foreign policy and international relations at the Library of Congress. He is a professor of political science and international affairs at George Washington University. Professor Goldgeier's areas of expertise include NATO, transatlantic relations, and U.S.-Russia relations. From 2001 to 2005, he directed the Institute for European, Russian, and Eurasian Studies at George Washington University.

Professor Goldgeier is coauthor of *Power and Purpose: U.S. Policy Toward Russia After the Cold War*, which received the 2004 Georgetown University Lepgold Book Prize in international relations. He has also authored *Not Whether But When: The U.S. Decision to Enlarge NATO* and *Leadership Style and Soviet Foreign Policy*, winner of the 1995 Edgar S. Furniss Book Award in national and international security.

Prior to joining the George Washington University faculty, Professor Goldgeier was an assistant professor at Cornell University, and he has been a visiting scholar at Stanford University, the Brookings Institution, the Woodrow Wilson Center, and the Hoover Institution. In 1995–96, he was a CFR international affairs fellow serving at the U.S. State Department and on the National Security Council staff. Professor Goldgeier graduated magna cum laude from Harvard University and received his PhD from the University of California, Berkeley.

Advisory Committee for
The Future of NATO

Robert John Abernethy
American Standard Development Co.

Peter Ackerman
Rockport Capital, Inc.

Zoltan Barany
University of Texas at Austin

Hans Binnendijk
National Defense University

Frank J. Caufield
Kleiner Perkins Caufield & Byers

Christopher Chivvis
RAND Corporation

Steven A. Cook
Council on Foreign Relations

James F. Dobbins
RAND Corporation

Karen Erika Donfried
*The German Marshall Fund
of the United States*

William M. Drozdiak
The American Council on Germany

Stephen J. Flanagan
Center for Strategic & International Studies

Daniel Hamilton
*Paul H. Nitze School of Advanced
International Studies*

Alexander S. Jutkowitz
Group SJR

F. Stephen Larrabee

Gale A. Mattox
U.S. Naval Academy

Kara C. McDonald
Council on Foreign Relations

Patricia Ann McFate
*Science Applications International
Corporation*

Jeremy D. Rosner
Greenberg Quinlan Rosner Research Inc.

Scott Schless
Defense Security Cooperation Agency

Stephen F. Szabo
*The German Marshall Fund
of the United States*

Kurt Volker
*Paul H. Nitze School of Advanced
International Studies*

Note: Council Special Reports reflect the judgments and recommendations of the author(s). They do not necessarily represent the views of members of the advisory committee, whose involvement in no way should be interpreted as an endorsement of the report by either themselves or the organizations with which they are affiliated.

Mission Statement of the International Institutions and Global Governance Program

The International Institutions and Global Governance (IIGG) program at CFR aims to identify the institutional requirements for effective multilateral cooperation in the twenty-first century. The program is motivated by recognition that the architecture of global governance—largely reflecting the world as it existed in 1945—has not kept pace with fundamental changes in the international system. These shifts include the spread of transnational challenges, the rise of new powers, and the mounting influence of nonstate actors. Existing multilateral arrangements thus provide an inadequate foundation for addressing many of today's most pressing threats and opportunities and for advancing U.S. national and broader global interests.

Given these trends, U.S. policymakers and other interested actors require rigorous, independent analysis of current structures of multilateral cooperation, and of the promises and pitfalls of alternative institutional arrangements. The IIGG program meets these needs by analyzing the strengths and weaknesses of existing multilateral institutions and proposing reforms tailored to new international circumstances.

The IIGG program fulfills its mandate by

- Engaging CFR fellows in research on improving existing and building new frameworks to address specific global challenges—including climate change, the proliferation of weapons of mass destruction, transnational terrorism, and global health—and disseminating the research through books, articles, Council Special Reports, and other outlets;
- Bringing together influential foreign policymakers, scholars, and CFR members to debate the merits of international regimes and frameworks at meetings in New York, Washington, DC, and other select cities;

– Hosting roundtable series whose objectives are to inform the foreign policy community of today's international governance challenges and breed inventive solutions to strengthen the world's multilateral bodies; and

– Providing a state-of-the-art Web presence as a resource to the wider foreign policy community on issues related to the future of global governance.

Council Special Reports

Published by the Council on Foreign Relations

The United States in the New Asia
Evan A. Feigenbaum and Robert A. Manning; CSR No. 50, November 2009
An International Institutions and Global Governance Program Report

Intervention to Stop Genocide and Mass Atrocities: International Norms and U.S. Policy
Matthew C. Waxman; CSR No. 49, October 2009
An International Institutions and Global Governance Program Report

Enhancing U.S. Preventive Action
Paul B. Stares and Micah Zenko; CSR No. 48, October 2009
A Center for Preventive Action Report

The Canadian Oil Sands: Energy Security vs. Climate Change
Michael A. Levi; CSR No. 47, May 2009
A Maurice R. Greenberg Center for Geoeconomic Studies Report

The National Interest and the Law of the Sea
Scott G. Borgerson; CSR No. 46, May 2009

Lessons of the Financial Crisis
Benn Steil; CSR No. 45, March 2009
A Maurice R. Greenberg Center for Geoeconomic Studies Report

Global Imbalances and the Financial Crisis
Steven Dunaway; CSR No. 44, March 2009
A Maurice R. Greenberg Center for Geoeconomic Studies Report

Eurasian Energy Security
Jeffrey Mankoff; CSR No. 43, February 2009

Preparing for Sudden Change in North Korea
Paul B. Stares and Joel S. Wit; CSR No. 42, January 2009
A Center for Preventive Action Report

Averting Crisis in Ukraine
Steven Pifer; CSR No. 41, January 2009
A Center for Preventive Action Report

Congo: Securing Peace, Sustaining Progress
Anthony W. Gambino; CSR No. 40, October 2008
A Center for Preventive Action Report

Deterring State Sponsorship of Nuclear Terrorism
Michael A. Levi; CSR No. 39, September 2008

China, Space Weapons, and U.S. Security
Bruce W. MacDonald; CSR No. 38, September 2008

Sovereign Wealth and Sovereign Power: The Strategic Consequences of American Indebtedness
Brad W. Setser; CSR No. 37, September 2008
A Maurice R. Greenberg Center for Geoeconomic Studies Report

Securing Pakistan's Tribal Belt
Daniel Markey; CSR No. 36, July 2008 (Web-only release) and August 2008
A Center for Preventive Action Report

Avoiding Transfers to Torture
Ashley S. Deeks; CSR No. 35, June 2008

Global FDI Policy: Correcting a Protectionist Drift
David M. Marchick and Matthew J. Slaughter; CSR No. 34, June 2008
A Maurice R. Greenberg Center for Geoeconomic Studies Report

Dealing with Damascus: Seeking a Greater Return on U.S.-Syria Relations
Mona Yacoubian and Scott Lasensky; CSR No. 33, June 2008
A Center for Preventive Action Report

Climate Change and National Security: An Agenda for Action
Joshua W. Busby; CSR No. 32, November 2007
A Maurice R. Greenberg Center for Geoeconomic Studies Report

Planning for Post-Mugabe Zimbabwe
Michelle D. Gavin; CSR No. 31, October 2007
A Center for Preventive Action Report

The Case for Wage Insurance
Robert J. LaLonde; CSR No. 30, September 2007
A Maurice R. Greenberg Center for Geoeconomic Studies Report

Reform of the International Monetary Fund
Peter B. Kenen; CSR No. 29, May 2007
A Maurice R. Greenberg Center for Geoeconomic Studies Report

Nuclear Energy: Balancing Benefits and Risks
Charles D. Ferguson; CSR No. 28, April 2007

Nigeria: Elections and Continuing Challenges
Robert I. Rotberg; CSR No. 27, April 2007
A Center for Preventive Action Report

The Economic Logic of Illegal Immigration
Gordon H. Hanson; CSR No. 26, April 2007
A Maurice R. Greenberg Center for Geoeconomic Studies Report

The United States and the WTO Dispute Settlement System
Robert Z. Lawrence; CSR No. 25, March 2007
A Maurice R. Greenberg Center for Geoeconomic Studies Report

Bolivia on the Brink
Eduardo A. Gamarra; CSR No. 24, February 2007
A Center for Preventive Action Report

After the Surge: The Case for U.S. Military Disengagement from Iraq
Steven N. Simon; CSR No. 23, February 2007

Darfur and Beyond: What Is Needed to Prevent Mass Atrocities
Lee Feinstein; CSR No. 22, January 2007

Avoiding Conflict in the Horn of Africa: U.S. Policy Toward Ethiopia and Eritrea
Terrence Lyons; CSR No. 21, December 2006
A Center for Preventive Action Report

Living with Hugo: U.S. Policy Toward Hugo Chávez's Venezuela
Richard Lapper; CSR No. 20, November 2006
A Center for Preventive Action Report

Reforming U.S. Patent Policy: Getting the Incentives Right
Keith E. Maskus; CSR No. 19, November 2006
A Maurice R. Greenberg Center for Geoeconomic Studies Report

Foreign Investment and National Security: Getting the Balance Right
Alan P. Larson and David M. Marchick; CSR No. 18, July 2006
A Maurice R. Greenberg Center for Geoeconomic Studies Report

Challenges for a Postelection Mexico: Issues for U.S. Policy
Pamela K. Starr; CSR No. 17, June 2006 (Web-only release) and November 2006

U.S.-India Nuclear Cooperation: A Strategy for Moving Forward
Michael A. Levi and Charles D. Ferguson; CSR No. 16, June 2006

Generating Momentum for a New Era in U.S.-Turkey Relations
Steven A. Cook and Elizabeth Sherwood-Randall; CSR No. 15, June 2006

Peace in Papua: Widening a Window of Opportunity
Blair A. King; CSR No. 14, March 2006
A Center for Preventive Action Report

Neglected Defense: Mobilizing the Private Sector to Support Homeland Security
Stephen E. Flynn and Daniel B. Prieto; CSR No. 13, March 2006

Afghanistan's Uncertain Transition From Turmoil to Normalcy
Barnett R. Rubin; CSR No. 12, March 2006
A Center for Preventive Action Report

Preventing Catastrophic Nuclear Terrorism
Charles D. Ferguson; CSR No. 11, March 2006

Getting Serious About the Twin Deficits
Menzie D. Chinn; CSR No. 10, September 2005
A Maurice R. Greenberg Center for Geoeconomic Studies Report

Both Sides of the Aisle: A Call for Bipartisan Foreign Policy
Nancy E. Roman; CSR No. 9, September 2005

Forgotten Intervention? What the United States Needs to Do in the Western Balkans
Amelia Branczik and William L. Nash; CSR No. 8, June 2005
A Center for Preventive Action Report

A New Beginning: Strategies for a More Fruitful Dialogue with the Muslim World
Craig Charney and Nicole Yakatan; CSR No. 7, May 2005

Power-Sharing in Iraq
David L. Phillips; CSR No. 6, April 2005
A Center for Preventive Action Report

Giving Meaning to "Never Again": Seeking an Effective Response to the Crisis in Darfur and Beyond
Cheryl O. Igiri and Princeton N. Lyman; CSR No. 5, September 2004

Freedom, Prosperity, and Security: The G8 Partnership with Africa: Sea Island 2004 and Beyond
J. Brian Atwood, Robert S. Browne, and Princeton N. Lyman; CSR No. 4, May 2004

Addressing the HIV/AIDS Pandemic: A U.S. Global AIDS Strategy for the Long Term
Daniel M. Fox and Princeton N. Lyman; CSR No. 3, May 2004
Cosponsored with the Milbank Memorial Fund

Challenges for a Post-Election Philippines
Catharin E. Dalpino; CSR No. 2, May 2004
A Center for Preventive Action Report

Stability, Security, and Sovereignty in the Republic of Georgia
David L. Phillips; CSR No. 1, January 2004
A Center for Preventive Action Report

To purchase a printed copy, call the Brookings Institution Press: 800.537.5487.
Note: Council Special Reports are available for download from CFR's website, www.cfr.org.
For more information, email publications@cfr.org.